La Ferme aux Grives (Photo Bieke Claessens)

With special thanks to our photographers

Bieke Claessens
Phile Deprez
Sven Everaert
Alain Machelidon
Patrick Verbeeck

&

Paul Kusseneers
Concept & Lay-Out

&

Printed by De Plano

Compiled by: Luc Quisenaerts
Concept & lay-out: Paul Kusseneers
Printed by: De Plano
Pre-press: Paul Kusseneers
Texts: Mia Dekeersmaeker
English translation: Anne&Owen Davis
French translation: Pancken Translations
German translation: Eva & Hans-Jürgen Schweikart
List of photographers:
Bieke Claessens: Château de Nieuil, Le Parc Victoria, Le Couvent des Herbes,Les Prés d'Eugénie & La Ferme
Thermale d'Eugénie, La Ferme aux Grives, La Maison Rose.
Phile Deprez: Château de Mercuès, Château de Roumegouse, Domaine de Rochebois, Château de Castel-Novel,
Le Manoir d'Hautegente, Château du Puy Robert, Château de la Treyne.
Sven Everaert: Domaine d'Auriac, L'Aubergade & Les Loges de l'Aubergade,
Michel Bras.
Alain Machelidon: Domaine d'Auriac.
Patrick Verbeeck: Château Cordeillan-Bages, Saint-James, Hôtel-Château Grand-Barrail, Domaine de Bassibé,
Le Chaufourg en Périgord, Le Vieux Logis, Château des Vigiers, Le Moulin de l'Abbaye, Le Moulin du Roc,
La Chapelle Saint-Martin, Château de Riell

ISBN 90-76124-16-7   D/1999/8101/3

First edition

Hidden gems of

DORDOGNE &
SOUTH WEST FRANCE

COMPILED

LUC QUISENAERTS

WRITTEN BY

MIA DEKEERSMAEKER

PUBLISHERS D-PUBLICATIONS

THE SERIES
Hidden gems

Dear reader,

In this series, we take you to the most wonderful places to stay, to eat and to enjoy the specialties of a country or an area.

Every article in this series is a journey of discovery, a unique revelation. We take a look behind the scenes in a hotel, a wine chateau, a restaurant where we savour the specialties of the chef or of the area…

With this series, we intend to give the readers the opportunity to leaf through each book and 'walk' through these wonderful spots, and discover the unique nooks and crannies of each of them.

Therefore this series, and each volume in itself, can be considered a valuable archive which brings a piece of the richness and beauty of an area or country into the home, created and cherished by the passion of the people who put part souls into it.

In word and photographs, the typical atmosphere of each place is conjured, and each book can be considered the 'key' to a wonderful and often undiscovered world.

The selection was made and approved of by the publisher himself, which guarantees it to be a unique experience, with unforgettable impressions of what our hosts have to offer.

. . .

Hidden gems of
DORDOGNE &
SOUTH WEST FRANCE

Hotels

I have seldom seen such a variety of scenery, seldom made so many discoveries while travelling. Discoveries in the way of beautiful landscapes, good cuisine and delightful hotels.

My journey led me through the fairytale beauty of Périgord and Quercy, a region scattered with intimate little villages and towns, nestled between green hills and impressive rocks, set beside tumbling rivers. This is a prehistoric area, with the caves of Lascaux as its highlight, but the Middle Ages and the Renaissance have also left their imprint here.

Just as fascinating as region is Pyrénées-Aquitaine, a mosaic of changing landscapes between the Atlantic Ocean and the Pyrenees.

From the Gironde delta, where grapes grow that produce the famous Bordeaux wines, I travelled south through the endless plains of Les Landes, as far as trendy St-Jean-de-Luz on the coast. And finally, I went east, into the Pyrénées Roussillon, past Carcassonne with its medieval walls, where a mediterranean atmosphere could be clearly felt.

On the way back, when I had almost completed a circle, I made an unexpected discovery in the Aveyron: the design temple of gastronomic delight of Michel Bras. My collection was complete: watermills that had been converted into hotels, castles, and estates with undulating golf courses, romantic mansions and farm houses, even a Victorian villa. And then, of course, there was that very special treat, unique in the world: the spa of Michel Guérard!

The only thing that remains to be said is: bon voyage…

Luc Quisenaerts
Publisher

THE COLLECTION

Château de Nieuil

Not far from Angoulême, capital of the beautiful Charente region, lies Château de Nieuil, between Limoges, renowned for its china, and Cognac, famous for its 'water of life'.

A long, tree-lined drive leads to an impressive Renaissance castle, set in lovely parkland. My eyes are like the lens of a camera: they take in every detail of the imposing building: the pointy turrets, the battlements, balustrades and balconies add a majestic touch to the glittering white façade. This is where the French King François I received his guests for hunting parties back in the sixteenth century.

Curious, I enter the large reception hall and discover an impressive spiral staircase; it leads up to ten rooms and three apartments. A stroll around them leads me, like a history book, from the sixteenth to the twentieth century. Richly decorated mantlepieces, giant gilded mirrors, impressive wooden panelling, wall-hangings and crystal chandeliers recall glorious days long gone. My attention is drawn to some exquisite pieces of furniture which are testimony to the craftsmanship of another era. Each room has its own personality and everything is carefully in keeping, from the wallpaper to the paintings. I especially love the Louis XVI room, looking out over the French gardens full of flowers, the meadows and the woods beyond. The garden is surrounded by a moat and there is a large pond for fishing in the park. Nearby, shaded by trees, are the swimming pool and the tennis courts. I'll visit the herb and vegetable gardens, but decide to have a glass of wine first, in the shade of the magnolia trees. Mrs. Luce Bodinaud tells me how important the gardens are for the castle: she and her assistant Pascal Pressac make extensive use of the vegetables and herbs in her tasty regional dishes. The Venetian dining room is as colourful and enchanting as the culinary delights that are served here. One of the many original touches at the castle is that the menu does-

n't offer the same dishes for lunch as for dinner. It doesn't surprise me that the Château de Nieuil has held a Michelin star since 1978. I savour the 'Farci de grand-mère Marie-Louise', an exquisite herb paté. It's a pity I'm on my own; groups of six to eight people can do workshops here and learn for themselves the secrets of these special recipes.

In the hall, Jean-Michel's extensive collection of cognacs takes pride of place. I reserve a number of bottles to take home, and plan to take a trip to Cognac tomorrow, and visit the Cognac house. Jean-Michel recommends a visit to one of his friends-producers of a fine variety. But first I will visit the art and antique gallery in the old stables of the castle. Luce has collected the beautiful pieces that can be seen here.

In my room, I throw open the windows and watch evening become night. The peacefulness, the lovely atmosphere and the beauty of the environment make my stay here unforgettable.

This is where King François I received guests
during his numerous hunting parties.

Le vieux Logis

My small garden at home is often neglected; there are simply too many other things to do. But when I see the colourful gardens of Le Vieux Logis, in the village of Trémolat in the Périgord Noir, on a bend of the river Dordogne, I realise how much there can be to enjoy in a beautiful and well-kept garden. Every day when I see the stunning view from my room, I decide that from now on, I will look after my own garden at home. This one has flowers, ferns of all kinds, fruit trees and vine-grown arches. Add to that the ivy-clad façade of the hotel and you're in a green paradise. Sitting under the trees, I can even see the green reflected in the water in my glass. Close by is a quiet stream, and a bit further on, down a beautiful pathway, lies the swimming-pool. Le Vieux Logis is very old. It was built on the remains of a burnt-down priory, and has been home to the Giraudel-Destord family for the last 400 years. The room where once tobacco was dried, built 180 years ago, where horses rested and the wines were kept, is now a restaurant offering a fine cuisine, prepared by the chef.

One of his specialities is 'Truffe en croûte' with a Perigeux sauce. The wooden cladding and the balcony from which you can see the restaurant from a different angle, refer to its former function. Red chairs and a flowery wallpaper with red as the main tone, give the room a special warm atmosphere. I find a similar richness of colours in the hotel rooms and in 'les logis des Champs', another suite of rooms set in a further building, that include an old coach house. Provençal materials from Souleïado and Canivas create a sunny and lively effect. The bathroom is like a small boudoir.

There is lots to do here: walking, cycling, canoeing, kayak trips, golf. Not far from the hotel is the wonderful Vieux Logis shop, which sells regional products. You can even book a trip in a hot air balloon or a helicopter. I choose the former, for the great view and the peacefulness. I am not surprised that Henry Miller, who once booked a room for a week here, ended up staying a month. It it wasn't for my garden at home, I'd be tempted to do the same.

L'Aubergade & Les Loges de l'Aubergade

L'Aubergade and Les Loges de l'Aubergade are synonymous with Michel and Marysse Trama, and vice versa. Michel Trama rules in the north of l'Agenais, Duc de Guyenne and de Quercy. Aubergade and the Logis constitute the palace, Puymirol is the capital. Michel is an eccentric, a hedonist, a sportsman, a culinary artist and lover of a good cigar. He communicates best through his cuisine. His dishes are a synthesis of the new and the traditional. Like an alchemist, he turns duck, poultry and truffles into dishes that delight all our five senses. His desserts are fireworks of colour and flavour.

His wines, such as the Bordelais and the old Armagnac, are in perfect harmony with his cuisine. At the end of the meal, he offers his guests a good cigar. Just like an artist, he makes sketches on paper of his dishes and creations before he cooks them.

His wife Marysse provides the perfect background for his art. She is an accomplished interior decorator, and works with respect for the traditions of l'Aubergade and the Logis, choosing from classical and baroque furniture, old paintings and Japanese etchings, leather, luxurious materials and inventive lighting. Her favourite colour is a deep blue, which can be found everywhere.

In Les Loges, traditional charm is combined with technological futurism. Everywhere, the graceful, colourful cherry is found as an emblem. Ten different kinds lend their names to the rooms. Each room is an oasis of peace. Whitewashed walls are integrated with bare bricks. Wooden beams give a rustic air. Windows and lighting play an intimate game with space.

My room has a very traditional atmosphere, but uses modern materials in such a way that the overall impression is one of harmony. This place is paradise. There is so much to discover: small sculptures of angels, cast

iron detailing, the Roman bath, the sunny terraces…

It is almost too good here to think of leaving to explore the countryside beyond. But there is plenty to discover, on foot, on horseback or by car… and, of course, all the beauty will still be waiting for you on your return.

First class design at its most original.

Château des Vigiers

This castle, also known as 'Little Versailles', can be found in the heart of the Périgord Pourpre, some 85 kilometres from Bordeaux and close to important vineyards such as Saint Emilion, Pomero, Sauternes, Médoc, Bergerac and Monbazillac. The imposing 16th century building has recently been renovated and is now a luxurious four star hotel. There are 25 rooms, decorated in the style of a French country house. A further 11 junior suites and 11 standard rooms were built close by, in traditional style, with ample use of brick and wood. The result is enchanting. Equally delightful are the regional specialities served in the gastronomic restaurant, 'Les Freques'. Duck, goose liver and truffles are always on the menu. For a choice of simpler, but no less succulent dishes, there is a brasserie, 'Le Chai'.

From the wide terrace, you have a breathtaking view across the golf course and the twinkling lake. But there is more. The sommelier will happily initiate you in the wine specialities of the castle. Merlot, Cabernet, Sauvignon, Sémillon and Muscadelle are wines from the area. Specialist Michel Rolland's knowledge of wines has won him a clutch of medals.

If you like golf, you don't have to go far. The castle is surrounded by an 18-hole course, par 72. Per Ulrik Johansson, who twice won the Ryder Cup and who is a member of the Château de Vigiers, really relishes the chal-

lenging course between plum trees, past the vineyards, the lake and the ancient wood with its sturdy old oak trees.

I am only an amateur myself; after a couple of hours' golf in the sunshine, I can feel my back. A perfect excuse, of course, to enjoy a massage and a beauty treatment. After that, I am relaxed enough to go for a cycle ride. I can see I'll have a busy time here: I want to go swimming, have a sauna, visit the steam room, enjoy the jacuzzi. There is also plenty to see in the area. The market towns of Sainte Foy la Grande and Bergerac, the caves of Lascaux in Montignac, a visit to the truf-

fle fields and the plethora of antique shops. But first, I have a good rest, with a favourite novel –tomorrow is another day. At 'Le Petit Versailles' I went to sleep like a princess. I feel utterly spoiled, and I know that I have the special atmosphere of the castle, and the friendly service of the staff to thank for it.

'Little Versailles' in the heart of the Périgord.

Le Moulin du Roc

In the heart of the Périgord Vert, on the banks of the river Dronne, some four miles from Brantôme, you will discover the Hotel Le Moulin du Roc. In the 17th century, this was a working mill, used for the production of sweet-smelling walnut oil. It has now been converted into a luxury hotel, where all your needs are met in the most stylish of ways.

Warm colours, beautiful furniture, ornamental ceilings, wooden structures which recall the original mill, beautiful mirrors and paintings – all contribute to the sheer delightfulness of the hotel's ten rooms and four apartments. Wherever you go, there is something to discover. Even the wine cellar is special, filled with carefully chosen French wines. At Le Moulin du Roc, a wine tasting is a delight for all the senses.

The same goes for the cuisine. Alain Gardillou presents his guests with the very best that the Périgord has to offer.

And then there are the gardens, a real oasis of every possible shade of green, interspersed with the most delightful flowers. Peace and clean air reign supreme. There are little bridges and steps in stone and wood, leading from the swimming pool to the tennis courts and other places of interest. They even bridge the river Donne, a paradise for fishing and boating.

There are beautiful walks to go on, castles and museums to be visited, caves to be investigated. More sporty types can practice go-karting, play golf on the 18-hole course, and go cycling. Alain and Maryse Gardillou receive their guests with discreet charm, and invites them to explore the exquisite gardens, enjoy the delightful and subtle lighting in the evening, smell the scents of the numerous flowers and savour the inventive cuisine. Le Moulin du Roc is a sheer delight, and a temporary home to share with friends.

'Le Moulin du Roc' is like a fairy tale.

Château Cordeillan-Bages

There are moments when you make a delightful discovery, and you suddenly feel that there are certain places on earth where life is more than worth living. The little town of Pauillac, in the middle of the Médoc, is one such place. It is a wine-growing region, but the sea plays an equally important part. When you enter the town, you immediately encounter the 17th century Château Cordeillan-Bages. The rectangular grey-white building with its impressive turreted entrance has changed hands many times through the ages. There was a time when it was sadly neglected, and fell into disrepair. In 1985, the Cazes family restored the estate with its extensive vineyards, to its original glory.

The fact that this four-star hotel is mentioned in the Relais et Châteaux guide is a guarantee of something rather special: its unique character, peacefulness and exceptional charm, and its exquisite cuisine.

The château has so much to offer. The classic interior is kept in various shades of red and green, reflecting the splendours of the surrounding countryside. Discreet lighting,

combined with natural light, give the hotel a charming and intimate atmosphere. The 25 rooms are spacious and have every modern comfort.

The south-facing dining room extends out onto a glorious terrace, with beautifully-kept gardens beyond. To eat in such an environment is a great pleasure, and at first I feel too much at peace right here to go off exploring. The château has a special treat in store for me: wine lovers, amateurs and experts alike, can take a five-day or a weekend course at the Ecole du Bordeaux and learn all there is to know about the famous Bordeaux wines. You learn how to taste and discuss the various wines and how to recognise the good ones. A visit to some of the most significant vineyards is also on the programme. Le Château Cordeillan-Bages is also on the Route des Châteaux. Of the 60 crus du Médoc that became 'classés' in 1855, 34 can be found less than 7 miles from the castle.

After all that, I need some relaxation, and there is plenty of opportunity for that in the area. 25 minutes away is the coast, where I can sunbathe, and three minutes from the hotel are a swimming pool and tennis courts. Golf lovers are no more than 30 minutes from the golf course of the Châteaux des Médocs.

Later, in the elegant restaurant, I can savour traditional regional cuisine and some excellent wines. The wine list is so extensive that I have to ask chef Thierry Marx and his team for advice.

The weather is wonderful, the shade of the plantains delightful. Before I know it, it has become very, very late. But here at the Château, far from the madding crowd, a peaceful and undisturbed night's sleep is assured.

Château de Mercuès

High above the river Lot lies a mansion that was once the home of the noble bishops of Quercy, now a beautiful hotel. Driving north from Toulouse, past the city of Cahors, I see at last the majestic Château de Mercuès rising high above me, on a precipice. This ancient residence of the noble bishops of Quercy seems to have withstood time and the passage of many generations. The morning mist that hangs over the river never reaches the parapet, and looking south on a clear day, you can see the faraway mountaintops of the Pyrenees. It was not without reason that Charles de Gaulle wrote on 26th May 1951: 'In Castle Mercuès, history was born'.

The historic monument of Mercuès became a fully-fledged Relais & Château hotel thanks to the passion of two men: Georges Héreil and Georges Vigouroux, the latter an important name in the wine industry in Cahors. Both took on the enormous task of restoring the castle. For ten long years, Vigouroux continued what Héreil had started; and finally under the terrace of the castle he built an impressive wine cellar.

Nowadays, there are 22 rooms and eight suites, all extremely comfortable, funished with antiques and offering luxurious bathrooms.

Each room has its own special flavour. There is, for instance, the room of the Bishop of l'Evêque (also Charles de Gaulle's room), which features a large bed of gilded wood and a bronze sundial set into the wooden floor. In the room called 'la Tour', the ceiling actually opens onto the sky. In order to reach 'La Tourelle', you follow a short private road; 'La Tour de Guet' can be reached via an intriguing spiral staircase. The terrace of l'Echauguette, in its turn, balances perilously over the river Lot. Add to all this the pleasant park, the hanging gardens, the beautiful outdoor swimming pool and the tennis courts… and you know that this is a place of sheer delight.

At your restaurant table, high over the river, you can choose from a menu featuring Mediterranean fish, local produce such as foie gras and Lalbenque truffles – the cuisine here is delightful and authentic, very clearly inspired by the very special surroundings.

Left: 'Château de Mercuès' has an impressive Roman-Byzantian wine cellar.

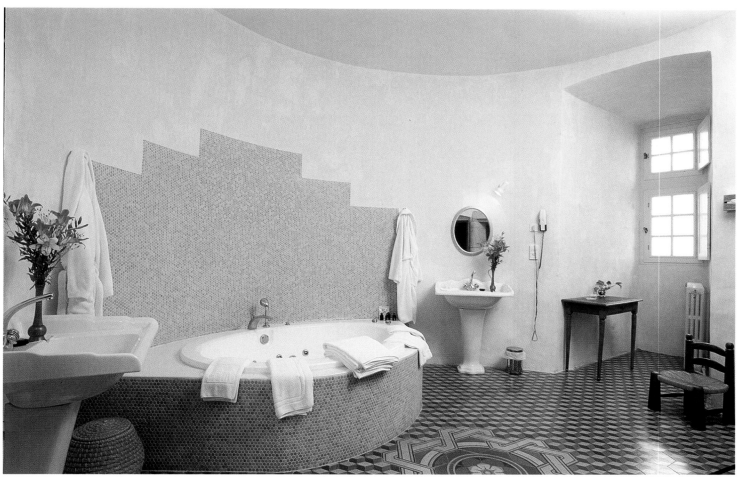

Saint-James

The Saint-James is situated on top of a hill, overlooking the Garonne valley, with Bordeaux and the pine woods of Les Landes off in the distance. The hotel was built on the foundations of a simple wine-grower's house, the central part of which goes back to the 17th century. Owner Jean-Marie Amat followed the professional advice of Jean Nouvel, architect of the Arabic Institute in Paris. The two men have a common taste for good food, quality wines and loyal friendship – a co-operation which has resulted in an hotel that would satisfy the most demanding of guests, perfectly intergrated into the environment, making clever use of light and perspective. The hotel is composed of four houses connected by an outside gallery, set in some lovely gardens. 18 large rooms offer beautiful views of the valley. Here, you are constantly surrounded by nature. The interior is simple and light, very Zen, with plaster walls, white wooden beds, made with white sheets, and matching furniture. The restaurant is Jean-Marie Amat's favourite place. His cuisine is like his hotel: simple and inventive. Eating here is always a voyage of discovery, where you find flavours and combinations ranging from the simple to the ingenious. His cooking is obviously influenced by his travels in Italy, the United States and China. The shelves full of Bordeaux wines are beautifully integrated into the restaurant; they look like a library of aromas and flavours. And Jean-Marie Amat keeps adding new projects. 'Le Bistroy' for instance, a meeting place for friends, decorated with simple, Spanish-looking materials, in a simple style. Serrano hams and sausages hang from the ceiling. Sushi, chilli and Chinese soups are examples of his fusion kitchen. A wall full of photographs by the celebrated Georges Fessy lend an extra dimension. 'Le Café de l'Espérence' is his third creation, continuing the success of the Saint-James and the Bistroy. Inside, the white wooden walls match the wooden tables. Outside, round white tables are set out under an arbour. The dishes here are as simple as the decoration. Soups, hors d'oeuvres and snacks are served in this gorgeous environment. Here, you find food for every mood - and for the soul.

High on a hill, with a beautiful view of the city of Bordeaux, lies the a world of Jean-Marie Amat.

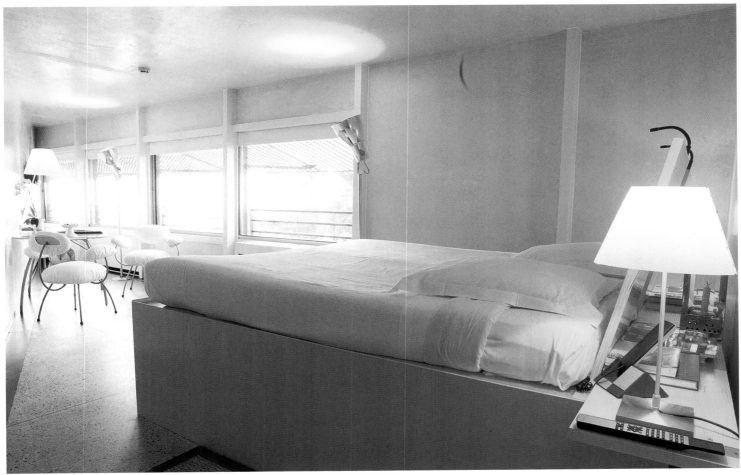

Le Domaine d'Auriac

Between the Mediterranean, the Montagne Noir and the Corbières, a stone's throw from the medieval town of Carcassonne, lies Domaine d'Auriac, surrounded by an ancient park, three centuries old. I get out of my car, tired from my long drive, and relish the peacefulness of the surroundings and the cool gardens. The house is built over the cellars of a former Carlovingian abbey, and I fall in love at once with its charmingly restored façade. I am greeted warmly at reception and immediately feel that all my dreams of dolce far niente and good food, mixed with touches of culture and exercise, will be fulfilled here. 26 comfortable rooms, each of them immaculately decorated, are spread across the main house, and the near-by houses named Boulanger, Meunier and l'Ecuyer. I am shown round by Anne-Marie and Bernard Rigaudis, and then taken to my room, which has a great view over the garden. It doesn't take me long to discover the swimming pool and the restaurant, furnished in exotic woods. I have my dinner by the pool and enjoy the last rays of sunshine of this fine summer day.

In the restaurant overlooking the golf course, the doors to the terrace are thrown open. The cuisine of Bernard Rigaudis offers regional dishes and his own specialities using goose liver, meat and fish. That same evening, on Anne-Marie's advice, I visit the medieval town, with its lustrous illuminations. It's like walking through a piece of history, and I am not surprised that Unesco has declared this part of the city a conservation area.

Next morning, I take a stroll in the Corbières countryside. The small road to

Forntiès leads along the ruins of the magnificent strongholds of Queyribus and Peyrepertuse, silent witnesses to a stormy past. On the way back, via Saint-Hilaire, I see the ruins of Château d'Auriac standing in the old feudal grounds of the count who

gave his name to the estate. Back at the hotel, I play a game of tennis, and later, in the restaurant, I enjoy a 'carré d'agneau piqué d'anchois de Collioure et les cannellonis d'aubergines', something of a mouthful, but delicious. Before I retire, I climb down into the cellars of the abbey, which have been renovated with due respect for its architectural history, and watch a little billiards, played with elan by two well-matched rivals. The following morning, I decide to try out the golf course. A professional golfer is on hand to offer me some good tips. Back at Le Domaine, I have lunch by the pool

and enjoy 'une salade d'été' and 'un melon glacé aux fruits de saison'. Only birdsong and the sound of crickets can be heard. I nod off in the shadow of the pine trees and I know that here, at Le Domaine d'Auriac, my wishes have all come true.

Le Couvent des Herbes, Les Prés d'Eugénie & La Ferme Thermale d'Eugénie

In the Dordogne area, between Bordeaux and Toulouse, near Mont-de-Marsan and Grenade-sur-l'Ardour, you can find the world of Michel and Christine Guérard, in the charming village of Eugénie-les-Bains. Michel is renowned for his low-calorie cuisine which offers taste, simplicity, slim-line dishes and utter refinement. Christine is famous for the diversity and refinement with which she has decorated 'Hotel Couvent des Herbes', the lovely 'Maison Rose' inn, the 'Ferme Aux Grives' guesthouse and the 'Ferme Thermale d'Eugénie' health centre. Each of these places is a treat in itself.

'Le Couvent des Herbes' was built in the 18th century. During the revolution the convent was badly damaged, but Napoleon III made sure it was carefully restored and dedicated the chapel to his wife, the Empress Eugénie. The Sisters of Béthanie, who lived here, spent their lives educating young ladies.

In 1986 the convent was bought by Christine Guérard's father. Since then, much has changed, but the vegetable garden is as charming as ever, and the roses wind themselves just as beautifully around the gallery of the convent as they did all those years ago. It took three years to convert the building into a guest house. The eight rooms have all been decorated differently, yet make a harmonious whole. Christine has used her favourite colours: lots of white, combined with sunny yellow, warm reds and blues. The upholstery is by Pierre Frey, and everything here shows Christine's personal touch: the bedheads, the drapes, the curtains, the antique furniture… Each room is named after a children's song. The ancient tiled floors are covered in beautiful rugs. In the fireplace, logs are waiting. Everywhere, you feel the peace and quiet that have always reigned in this beautiful building.

Then there is 'Les Prés d'Eugénie', which the Guérard family acquired some twenty years ago. This white colonial palace with its 35 rooms and apartments is surrounded by elegant gardens, and is situated near Eugénie-les-Sources. The modern 'Ferme Thermale d'Eugénie' is the result of 30 years' work by Michel and Christine. The house, which is kept in authentic rural style, has a beautiful bust of Eugénie in the hallway – very suitable, in view of the fact that Napoleon's wife was a pioneer when it came to beauty treatments. Inside, everything breathes calm and beauty. The materials and colours that have been used reflect nature itself; The baths are very important here, and Celtic, Greek-Latin and oriental touches can be found everywhere. There are log fires which exude the fragrant scents of herbs, a heated marble treatment table, beautiful flower arrangements, linen and cotton materials. Michel developed a unique recipe for a beautifying bath, and emulsion of kaolin and thermal water, soft as a cream, soothing and cleansing. After that, a thermal shower refreshes you completely, and then it is time to relax on a bed with a natural-fibre mattress. Or you could meditate, and enjoy a glass of fragrant tea with thyme, lemon, eucalyptus and honey. Such delicious herb cocktails are another trademark of 'La Ferme Thermale d'Eugénie'.

A bust of Empress Eugénie welcomes you
into the hall of 'La Thermale d'Eugénie',
built in rural regional style.

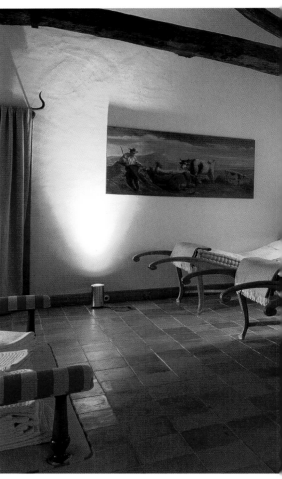

La Maison Rose

In the Gascogne region, in the charming little town of Eugénie-les-Bains, which is well-known for its thermal baths, a magnificent lawyer's office has been converted inventively and sympathetically into an exceptional hotel. A pink façade, decorated with small white violets, seems to invite the guest to enter. Inside the Maison Rose, the atmosphere is British, with French touches.

Numerous charming details, all over the house, make this a very special, utterly refined home away from home. And it is all due to owner Christine Guérard, who does everything within her power to make her guests feel special. She surprises them with bouquets of freshly-cut flowers, with pots full of fragrant herbs and with baroque dishes laden with apples and lemons.

On the ground floor, the restaurant and the lounge are decorated in a radiant, joyful yellow. White wood panelling and soft lights create a very special atmosphere here.

The rooms are decorated in peaceful pastel colours. The furniture and the many decorative objects have been chosen carefully by Christine herself. When it comes to interior decoration, Christine is constantly striving for perfection.

Perfection is also the only word to describe the fine dishes prepared by her husband, Michel Guérard. His delicious 'menus minceur' are prepared from superb secret recipes all his own. Don't forget to taste one of his wonderful drinks, prepared from hand-picked herbs. And if you want to know more, you can take classes with him in the spring and in the autumn, and learn how to cook 'Cordon bleu minceur'.

A stay at the 'Maison Rose', with its wonderful swimming pool behind the house, is a very special experience. The term 'cocooning' could have been invented here, 'Dolce far niente' is at the order of the day.

71

Christine Guérard has always strived for perfection in the decoration of her hotels.

La Ferme aux Grives

Autumn 1859. The beautiful Empress Eugénie, wife of Napoleon III, was travelling through Gascogne, and at nightfall reached a charming village, now known as Eugénie-les-Bains. Together with her ladies-in-waiting, each more beautiful than the other, she sought refuge at 'La Ferme aux Grives', the only inn in the village. The royal party settled down by the log fire and enjoyed an improvised meal.

Today, that very inn has been restored to its former glory, thanks to its owners Michel and Christine Guérard. These days, there are just four different guest rooms, with the enchanting names of 'Petit Jardin', 'Joli Matin', 'Bleu Palombe' and 'Pomme Reinette'. Visitors can stay here for a minimum of two nights – but once they have settled in, they will surely want to stay much longer. In 'Joli Matin', the four-poster bed is upholstered in Pierre Frey material, which gives a romantic touch to the room. Breakfast in bed would seem tempting here, but the alternative is even more appealing. Breakfast is served in the rural 'chocolaterie' on a 17th-century Castilian table The interior is like a Provençal kitchen.

The 'Salon des Demoiselles' is equally attractive, with genuine Louis XVI chairs, beautifully restored and re-upholstered, again, with Pierre Frey materials. Crockery from the era of Charles X and Napoleon III stands on shelves behind the glass doors of built-in cupboards,.

The garden is another delight. In the large vegetable garden at 'La Ferme aux Grives' apple and pear trees grow alongside fragrant herbs. There are lettuces and cabbages, roses

and shrubs. The inner courtyard is another treat, with climbing roses, wild thyme, laurel trees and potted plants. Cast-iron tables and chairs invite you to sit down and savour the silence here. In this historic inn, time – at least for a while – seems to stand still.

This rural inn from 1815 has completely retained its original atmosphere and charm.

Le Parc Victoria

Saint-Jean-de-Luz is a delightful historic town in the Basque region; it offers the visitors a wealth of things to do: sports, a host of cultural activities, delightful boutiques, excellent local cuisine, and a warm, pleasant climate.

It is situated on the Basque coast, and the bay with its beach and its picturesque little harbour has a real holiday feel to it.

Just as delightful is the hotel 'Le Parc Victoria', not just because of its unique Victorian architecture, but also because of its beautiful interiors. Eight rooms and four suites, each with its own garden, have all been decorated in a different style, with art deco-inspired furniture.

The two floors in the main building have an impressive staircase and an elevator. The fine marble bathrooms are the height of luxury. From my window, I have a breathtaking view of the park; thick with trees,

That are like natural parasols, plants of every kind, shrubs, colourful beds of gorgeous summer flowers and a beautiful lawn make this a wonderful place for a long and leisurely stroll. When I take a deep breath, I can smell perfumes even the most distinguished perfume houses could never recreate.

The "Les Lierres" restaurant, near the swimming pool, is elegant and peaceful, a perfect place for a leasurely meal. The tables are tastefully laid, with tablecloths, plates and glasses decorated with ivy leaves, in beautiful harmony with the view of the park.

The young chef Olivier Millet has an inventive way with tuna, turbot and the freshest of local vegetables.

After an excellent meal, I find even more tranquility as I stroll at the very edge of the waves on the beach beneath the hotel.

Later on, I take part in deep-sea diving, and after that, I enjoy a thalasso therapy treatment.

From my balcony, at bedtime, I watch the full moon and listen to the sounds of nature. Cast-iron lanterns illuminate the garden and create a very special atmosphere. Tomorrow, I will hire a jeep and go exploring in the magnificent Basque countryside.

The interior is like an opulent living room in a private home.

Le Moulin de l'Abbaye

Le Moulin de l'Abbaye, by the side of a river, is a place full of romance.

As a child, I was fascinated by windmills. Their architectural shape and the way the sails played with the elements of nature, intrigued me. School trips to areas with working examples of this phenomenon were of great interest to me, and articles on mills converted to houses still fascinate me. And so I didn't take much persuading to go to idyllic Périgord, on the banks of the river Dronne. Especially since I knew I would find a mill there with sails that still went round. The river embraces the medieval little town of Brantôme. Of five bridges here that span the Dronne, the 16th century one is the oldest and most beautiful. Close by, lies the mill of Brantôme, now called Moulin de L'Abbaye. Both the mill and the granary belonging to the abbey, right opposite, were converted by Cathy Bulot and now make up an enchanting hotel with 17 rooms and three apartments. The atmosphere is cosy. My room, 'Château Haut-Brion', is decorated in typical Provençal style, with rich reds and greens in perfect harmony with each other. The four-poster bed, the softly-coloured curtains, the cane chairs with their check cushions, the enchanting decorative wooden objects - everything is delightful here. An eye for detail, attention to creature comforts, and the fine materials used, are features of all the rooms, each of which is named after a 'grand cru classé du Bordelais'. For the restaurant, Cathy Bulot has chosen lively colours. Both the ceiling, by Pierre Frey, and the walls are an explosion of different shades of cheerful yellow. The blue and yellow crockery on the tables are reminiscent of Claude Monet's dining room in Giverny.

Just as enchanting are the meals that are served here. The quiet terrace overlooking the Dronne, with Brantôme in the distance is an utterly peaceful place to sit and relax. I take a boat trip on the river, and see the landscape from a completely different viewpoint. Later, I stroll through the romantic medieval streets of Brantôme, looking longingly into the windows of the antique shops; I visit the medieval tower of Château de Bourdeilles, which dates from the Renaissance, and admire the fascinating collection

of Spanish and Burgundian furniture from the 16th and 17th century, the beautiful paintings and wall-hangings. Eventually, I am tired enough to start longing for my mill. Late that night, one of my childhood dreams comes true: I fall asleep to the murmur of water and the sound of the creaking sails of the mill.

Château de Puy Robert

About a mile from the friendly little town of Montignac, on the banks of the river Vézère, lies Château de Puy Robert. Its towers cast shadows on the white bricks of the façade which are so typical of the Périgord Noir region. The reflections in the many windows of this neo-Renaissance building are nothing short of magical. I meet the amiable Vincent and Isabelle Nourisson, who are responsible for this utterly enchanting castle, and who tell me something of its long history and the story of its restoration. I can feel immediately this will be a place to relax completely. François Mittérand, princess Galyani of Thailand, James Coburn and many other famous visitors have no doubt felt the same. It doesn't surprise me to hear that this is a favourite haunt of the Dalai Lama.

Take the dining room, bathing in the sunshine that streams through the high windows... it's a very peaceful place., with an enchanting view of the large park. Birds, squirrels, pheasants, rabbits and foxes populate this paradise.

For gourmets, paradise can be found on the plate too, thanks to the tasty cuisine of chef Laurent Dufour. His culinary art was rewarded with stars as long as ten years ago, and rightly so. His dishes are inspired by traditional cuisine, but are given his personal accent. He uses fresh produce and wine which he obtains direct from local suppliers. Monbazilllac, Cahors and some great Bordeaux wines are all on offer here.

After dinner, there is time for a quiet drink in the bar or in one of the two cosy lounges. It would be hard to choose a favourite from the five luxury suites upstairs: they are all equally comfortable and romantic, but each of them is differently decorated. There are

attic rooms as well, where you can sleep under the stars.

I choose a room in the small manor house not far from the castle, if only for the romantic balcony with its view across the swimming pool.

After a good night's sleep and an extensive breakfast, I decide to visit the legendary caves of Lascaux, for which Montignac is justly famous. After only a quarter of an hour's walk I seem to have arrived in the middle of prehistoric times. Fascinated, I study the cave drawings with their clever use of perspective and finely observed details. On the way back, I look around me with different eyes. Full of respect, I remember the artists among the Cro-Magnons and the world they knew and recorded so well. The weather is lovely and warm, and I feel like a cooling swim in the pool. Floating on my back, I look up at the clouds, finding shapes and figures in them, like I did as a child.

That evening, I choose the seven-course Lascaux menu. Afterwards, I curl up in a red armchair and sip an exceptional Armagnac. I feel no more need to go exploring. The tennis court and a canoe trip down the river Vézère will have to wait until tomorrow. Right now, I'm in heaven.

La Chapelle Saint-Martin

Hotel la Chapelle Saint-Martain in Nieul is a welcoming oasis.

The china coffee service betrays the close proximity of the celebrated town of Limoges. The whole neo-classical hotel seems to bathe in the most wonderful of colours. In some rooms, yellow and blue dominate, with just the odd touch of red. An enormous verandah links the interior, with its beautifully soothing atmosphere, to the lush green world outside. The hotel lies in the middle of vast woods and is surrounded by a park with lawns and flower beds. Everywhere, small paintings and elegant sculptures catch the eye; there are original little touches throughout the hotel.

In the restaurant, the menu looks extremely tempting, with various kinds of fish and beautifully fresh meat and vegetables, ingredients in a range of regional dishes. Not surprising, if you know the reputation of chef Gilles Dudognon, who has earned himself several Michelin stars.

Armed with a towel and a bathrobe, I head for the swimming pool; which has been beautifully integrated into the landscape. Afterwards, warm and glowing, I decide to set off on a voyage of discovery. I drive through the green landscape where cows gaze at me curiously as I go by. I catch sight of fishermen on the river Vienne, and stop at the lake of Saint-Pardoux where I sit by the mirror-like water. I bend forward and clearly see my own reflection, and think of fairy-tales with frogs that change into princes. Who knows, if I wait long enough…

But I'm thirsty, and I turn back at last to the hotel and settle myself on the verandah. The chef himself chooses an excellent wine for me, and while I sip it, I watch the softly waving trees, and listen to the leaves that rustle in the soft breeze. I remember what I read earlier: that Hilary Clinton spent a couple of hours here, on her way to visit Bernadette Chirac. Maybe she sat in exactly the same place as I am now.

Château de la Treyne

Sometimes, life is a dream come true. When you first set eyes on Château de la Treyne, in the glow of the setting sun, is such an instance. The setting is utterly romantic: the castle stands, like a fairy tale, high on a rock overlooking the river Dordogne in south west France.

It was built back in 1342. During the 100 year war and the religious wars that were fought here, the castle was partly burnt down and destroyed. But during the reign of Louis XIII, it was restored to its former glory and these days, the castle is as elegant and impressive as ever.

Michèle Gombert, the owner, is passionate about the place, and she makes certain that everything here is of an utter refinement and elegance. There is, for instance, an official Louis XIII reception room, which has remained unchanged for centuries. You will feel like royalty when you stay in one of the 14 rooms and apartments which either look out on the beautiful gardens with their old Lebanese cedar trees, or onto the river, where the sunset is at its most stunning. On that side of the building, the Louis XIII room with its four-poster bed can be found, as well as the Vendanges room, named after the fine local Cahors wine. The latter, by the way, is situated in a tower which was once used as a prison…

There is plenty to see in the area: prehistoric Les Eyries, or the caves of La Cave and Lascaux with the world famous cave painings, for instance. The towns of Sarlat and Rocamadour, both equally stunning, surrounded by a beautiful landscape of hills and chalky rocks. Or you could visit the Bastides, beautiful fortified garrison towns, where street markets offer endless delights such as foie gras, truffles and tasty local wines. But the most surprising voyage of culinary discovery can be made at the castle itself, where the chef prepares the most succulent dishes for privileged guests. When the weather permits, the meals are served on the roomy terrace with its view of the river. Château de la Treyne is a place of utter romance, by day and by night.

Top: a unique location above the river Dordogne.

After the religious wars, the castle was restored to its original glory during the reign of Louis XIII.

Michel Bras

When you approach Laguiole in Aveyron, the scenery suddenly changes. The countryside becomes more peaceful, but the light gets brighter and more lively. The endless stretches of meadowland, divided by long beech hedges are as fascinating as the 'burons', old shepherds' houses with roofs that seem almost to touch the ground. This is Aubrac.

The earth here is full of granite and basalt. This is a rough and desolate area, seemingly forgotten by man. But Michel Bras is fascinated by its atmosphere and authenticity. Both he and Ginette Bras were born here, and they felt so at one with this environment that they chose to stay. Their hotel, like the wild surroundings, shows its beauty only gradually. They are strong believers in the principle that Aubrac should be discovered bit by bit.

The architecture of the buildings is simple and strict, integrated skilfully into the surroundings in a pure and modern way. The materials themselves come from the area. The restaurants seems somehow to float in the air and disappear into the landscape, and even in the heart of winter you have the odd impression that you are dining outside. The lounge, which has windows along every wall, gives the impression that you are sitting in a castle in the air. It's the perfect place to enjoy an after-dinner drink.

Each of the rooms are very different. Most of them offer impressive views of unspoilt nature and bathe in the bright light of Aubrac. Tucked away in the rolling landscape, they offer guests a great measure of intimacy, a feeling that they are staying in surroundings that seem to have been created just for them.

Le Manoir d'Hautegente

Far from the main road, between the valley of la Vézère and the valley of the Dordogne, in the heart of the Périgord Noir, lies the estate of 'Manoir d'Hautegente'. The façade is covered in ivy, which contrasts beautifully with the grey slates of the roof. Nearby, on the river, is a 13th-century watermill which once served the house, but now only the foundations remain. Old buildings beyond were once a farmhouse, but today only house a gaggle of geese.

The decoration of the bedrooms is inspired by archive material from the time of Louis XVI: antique furniture, parquet floors and brightly-coloured carpets create a cosy atmosphere. Red and green are the main colours, in perfect harmony with the view over the green gardens, planted with a host of flowers. The 14 rooms in 'Le Manoir d'Hautegente' all have garden views.

I wander around the ground floor, from the dining room to the intimate lounges. Small tables, beautifully laid, set about with candles and antique chairs, stand in the rooms, their charm enhanced by the wooden mantlepieces in typical Périgord style. A Louis XIV sideboard with three drawers takes pride of place in the hall, and what once was a forge is now a cosy Louis XIII lounge.

The weather is lovely, as the sun begins its slow decline, the skies become soft and velvety. It's time for dinner, so I choose a table out on the beautifully lit terrace. The sound of the slow and peaceful river close by, inspires me to choose the 'lasagne de cabillaud aux chanterelles'. Delicious!

If you like trout fishing, this river is the place to go. I prefer the heated swimming pool. Afterwards, after a hot shower, I stand at my window, a glass of Puy Servain rouge in hand, and listen to the concert of the rustling trees. It is utterly peaceful and quiet here.

That night, I have a deep and dreamless sleep, and awaken to birdsong, and lots of plans for the day ahead.

'Le Manoir d'Hautegente', a hidden jewel in the heart of the Périgord.

Le Château de Roumegouse

A turbulent history, the remains of a rampart, a beautiful array of turrets, a terrace full of parasols and a swimming pool are the main ingredients of this Château. Add to that its location in the lovely northern part of the Lot province, called Le Quecy, and you realise that this is the most natural and harmonious part of the famous Dordogne valley. On the map, Rocamadour, once known as the way of the pilgrims to St. Jacques de Compostelle and distant Rome, is my point of reference. Le Château de Roumegouse is set on a hill, in the middle of a green park. My room in this gothic renaissance castle has the most magnificent view. Antique furniture, paintings, carefully draped materials on the walls - all part of the very individual charm of each room. The

owners, Luce and Jean-Louis Laîné, happily let their guests share the objects that are so dear to them: favourite antiques, sculptures, paintings and souvenirs. The castle has been pleasantly decorated, in a comfortable, easy style. The library with its round walls, wooden beams, blue, red and brown colours has a very historical feel. The reading material is varied: from heavy books to comics. There are fresh flowers everywhere - Luce's speciality. Jean-Louis is a talented cook, with a penchant for traditional dishes and local ingredients. Dinner is served in three different places. Since the weather is so clement, I decide to eat out on the terrace, amongst the white geraniums. This romantic old castle is strategically placed for all kinds of trips and outings. In the summer months, there are

concerts in Rocamadour, Martel and Gramat, with the festival of opera in Saint-Céré an unmissable event. Towns like Carennac, Sarlat and Rocamadour are perfect for a cultural stroll with a spot of shopping as a bonus. I take a kayak trip on the river Lot. I arrive back at the castle, tired but relaxed, and walk to my room through the park. That night, accompanied by candle light and soft music, I enjoy a three-course meal with a red Cahors wine from one of the oldest wine regions in France.

Le Domaine de Bassibé

Walking along one of the boundaries of Les Landes and Gers, I pass down narrow roads bordered by cornfields and hedgerows full of wild flowers. While I proceed, I softly practice the three syllables: Bas-si-bé. According to the legend, this melodious name means 'a place where one feels happy'. An apt name for a delightful family home. Through the years, what once was a grand farmhouse grew into a rural relais, presently the only Relais & Châteaux hotel in the province of Gers. It gives me a perfect opportunity to discover the mellow life of the Gasconne area. A wooden sign written in elegant calligraphy letter invites me to follow a drive lined with majestic chestnut and laurel trees. They accompany me all the way to small red-roofed houses grouped around an old 18th century central building. The young owners, Sylvie and Olivier Lacroix, greet me with warm enthusiasm. They lead me on a guided tour through the natural wild garden with its gorgeous flowers, towards 'La Maison des Champs'. The rooms and suites here are wonderful, each of them different, with clever use of colour, furniture and opulent materials. They exude the taste and personality of the owners. Family heirlooms, books, photographs and paintings create an impression that you are staying with friends, not in an hotel at all.

I unpack and set out to explore the surroundings. The garden, dominated by impressive trees, some of them well over a century old, is full of surprises. Clematis, masses of roses, mimosa and a fragrant old wistaria grow in the unorderly order that only nature can provide. Everything is a delight here: the bar with its terrace, the swimming pool, an enormous oak tree nearby that gives welcome shade, and the magnificent view across the Gers valley. Chef Olivier Lacroix and his team echo in their cuisine the vast richness of the area, with succulent dishes cooked with great respect for fresh local produce. The extensive wine and liquor list invites me to taste products of the surrounding vineyards; names such as Madarin, Tursan, Côtes de Saint-Mont, Juraçon and of course the best Armagnacs are included. Visits to vineyards and wine tastings in this beautiful area can be arranged on request, and the owners will gladly advise you about the numerous other activities available. Afterwards, certain of the guests stroll through the lounge, spread out on an sofa, light up and bask contentedly in the delicious aroma of their real Havana cigars.

After a restful night's sleep, I have breakfast served in my room, as requested, at an hour that suits me. The time to leave has come far too soon. When I leave this place of peace, contentment and lovely food, I realise that the kindness of Sylvie and Olivier and their team is very special. I have found friends here.

128

'Le Domaine de Bassibé' is composed of a main building from the 18th century, and several smaller houses.

Château de Castel Novel

Limoges is the capital of the Limousin region and is famous for its beautiful china. Close by, in Pompadour, a castle was built for the mistress of Louis IV, known as the Marquess of Pompadour. She was a patron of the arts, sponsored artists and writers, and bred Anglo-Arabic horses. Soon, a race course was added to the property. And even today, all these years later, from July to mid-September, numerous activities are planned here, all open to the public.

My journey leads me a hundred kilometres further south, to the Château de Castel-Novel. The journalist and politician Henri de Jouvenel used to live here with Colette, the tramp-turned-novelist.

The light brown bricks of the façade and the black roof are in sharp contrast to the varied greenery surrounding the castle. Sturdy, ivy-clad turrets, charming little balconies and terraces enhance the solid character of the building, which was a significant stronghold during the turmoil of the Middle Ages.

Later, the castle became the property of people like d'Aubusson de la Feuillade, and began to play an important role in the politics of Vicomté. The atmosphere here must have inspired Colette as she wrote her numerous novels.

When I arrive, tired after my long drive, I am glad to rest a while and freshen up. The hotel has thirty rooms. And everywhere something reminds me of the fact that it is really a castle: the stone spiral staircases, the historic wall hangings, the wooden beams that seem almost to have been placed randomly in the rooms.

My room is done up mostly in pink. The small balcony looks out across the estate and into the countryside beyond. The woods are beautiful; some forty different varieties of oak trees can be found here. Ask the proud owner of the castle, Albert Parveaux, for a guided tour of the grounds; he will tell you all about his specialist oak collection.

The park features a swimming pool, tennis courts, and a three-hole practice golf course. Better players can go to one of the two 18-hole courses a convenient drive from the Château.

133

In the lounge, light streams in through the high windows. I'm looking forward to lunch, for Château de Castel-Novel is well-known for its culinary delights. Various dishes on the menu remind me of Colette, and I simply have to choose the 'menu Colette', accompanied by great wines from the local region. After a succulent meal, I wholeheartedly agree with what culinary specialist Marc de Champérard has said about the restaurant: 'C'est bon, délicat et bien pensé'. To the accompaniment of a glass of Saussignac, I savour patisserie 'La Flognarde', from an original recipe of Colette herself. Georges Pompidou, the French president, was so impressed that he took the recipe back to Paris.

After my meal, I sit down in the shadow of

one of the trees and bury my head in a
novel, – by Colette, of course. And I
completely forget all my plans for the after-
noon.

Le Domaine de Rochebois

As a journalist, I always like to find a peaceful place to write. Even when on holiday, I always have a pen and paper close by. The little desk in my hotel room offers a beautiful view of the magnificent Dordogne valley. In 1987, Doctor Louis Van de Walle saw this sleepy estate amongst the green oak trees and age-old chestnuts in the Périgord Noir, and he was fascinated by it. Together with his wife, he decided to awaken this Sleeping Beauty. The house was painstakingly and beautifully restored and in 1993, the 'Domaine de Rochebois' was opened. Nowadays, this four star hotel in charming neo-classical style is one of those places that remain in your memory for their discreet charm and peaceful harmony. The sunny entrance hall is made magnificent by the discreet lighting and the beautiful marble floor. In the park, all the beauty of the Villa Louise and the Pavillion Hortense is recaptured. Here at the 'Domaine de Rochebois', having breakfast al fresco in the fresh Perigord air, and watching the sun go down over the Dordogne Valley create memories of pure magic. It is hardly surprising that many famous people have already stayed in this celebrated hotel.

It is very relaxing to stroll through the gardens, and listen to the soft chuckle of fountains, inhaling the scent of honeysuckle and delicate jasmine. There is also a 9-hole golf course, perfectly integrated into the land-scape. It all seems so peaceful: the quiet banks of the Dordogne with the green hills beyond.

There is plenty of choice of how to spend the day. You can have a glass of wine in the English-style bar, or take a cooling swim in the pool. I choose the latter, and then take in the sunshine on the white terrace. In the evening, there is dinner in the hotel restaurant to look forward to. Chef Christophe Ochler likes using local produce in his cuisine, which is mentioned in two of the best culinary guides: Gault Millau and Champérard. Life at 'Le Domaine de Rochabois' is dolce far niente at its very best!

On the banks of the river Dordogne stands this wonderful golfers' hotel.

Château de Riell

Phone calls, letters, faxes, deadlines to meet and family problems to solve —sometimes life gets too hectic. At those moments, I feel a great need to retreat into a universe of peace and quiet, where I can find serenity in a harmonious environment.

The brochure for Molitg-les-Bains doesn't only look tempting, it also features the sentence: 'La Magie du Plancton Thermal pour votre beauté', conjuring up images of delightfully refreshing and restoring baths. My mind is made up. For a few days, the castle will become my private little world.

Under the warm Catalan sun, in the middle of the Roussillon, a few miles from Perpignan, completely surrounded by pine, oak and palm trees, it is an impressive castle, with a romantic turret. The interior is straight out of a fairy tale, full of captivating details such as rustic wooden ceilings, the gothic shape of the open doorways, the rural open fire in the dining room and the fresh light colours complementing the baroque wallpaper in the bedrooms. My bathroom is a small palace in itself, and the view out to the horizon couldn't be more relaxing.

This is the 'inland' Mediterranean, with the Pyrenees close by.

After a visit to the hotel doctor, who supplies me with masses of practical information, I begin my programme of relaxation and pampering. I have mainly chosen treatments to restore my energy and reduce my stress levels.

In the morning, there is a strengthening and cleansing thermal bath with plankton, taken in the beautiful Roman vaults... not just beneficial for the skin, but also good for my breathing and a treatment for rheumatism. After that, I feel fit enough for some swimming and a game of tennis. Later, by car, I visit Prades, where the famous Pablo Casals festival is held every year, then follow the route from Marquixanes to Arbousols. The beautiful views of the valley of the Têt and the Canigou are worth it in themselves.

That evening I enjoy a candle-lit dinner, feeling physically tired, but totally relaxed mentally.

Afterwards, I sip a glass of wine, lying in a hammock, with a romantic view of the castle and its surrounding buildings. When it gets a little chilly outside, I return to one of the cosy armchairs in the lounge. This, indeed is a very special castle. As the brochure says: 'beauty is a daily affair here'.

An enchanting interior.

Hôtel-Château Grand Barrail

A stone's throw from the medieval town of Saint-Emilion, some thirty minutes' drive from Bordeaux, you will find the unique Hotel Château Grand Barail, surrounded by vineyards. The name itself has something of a noble ring, and the building, with its numerous turrets is an impressive example of early 19th century architecture.

The house was built for a certain Mr. Bouchard, its structure based on a castle he owned in St. Amand les Eaux near Valenciennes.

The castle has been beautifully renovated, with due respect for its auspicious past, and has now become a restaurant and five-star hotel. Romantic rooms, enchanting interiors in the softest of pastel colours, original stained-glass windows and ceramic frescoes all contribute to the special atmosphere at the Grand Barail.

All the 23 rooms and 5 spacious suites offer beautiful views of the large park with its heated open-air swimming pool and the vineyards of Saint-Emilion. Some of them have their own balcony or terrace.

Since it opened, hotel Château Grand Barail has been a mecca for lovers of good wine and gourmet food. Chef Philippe Etchebest, who was born locally, serves the most regal of cuisine, prepared with local produce and

a great deal of creativity and inventiveness. His favourite dish, 'Lasagne de foie gras aux champignons des bois, émulsion de truffes noirs' is a delight. The wine list is equally impressive, with more than 450 wines, from wines from Saint Emilion, Pomerol and Montagne to old and prestigious wines such as a 1970 Château Ausone or a 1986 Cheval Blanc. I chose a bottle of Lamarzelle-Fignac, a wine from vineyards opposite the castle. The hotel, by the way, has a special room for wine tasting, where guests are only allowed in the company of the hotel's sommelier or a professional wine expert. But there is much more to see in the area. The friendly staff of Hotel Château Grand Barail will be more than happy to help you plan a special outing to your taste, whether you are interested in history, architecture or sports.

Le Chaufourg en Périgord

After many years travelling the world as a succesful fashion photographer and journalist Georges Dambier came home, to the house where he spent wonderful holidays as a child, and made it into an hotel full of poetry. The gorgeous 17th century building in the typical Périgord style can be found just outside the town of Sourzac. Like an immense terrace, it overlooks an idyllic island in the river Isle. The poetry starts in the rooms. Each of them named after memorable women and children who, over the years, crossed his path, and each of them has its own particular character. There is, for instance, 'Marie', a stunning suite in blue, with white beams and a lovely view of the river, or 'Guillaume', with its spiral staircase and an attic window looking out on magnolia trees and the swimming pool. 'Françoise' has a balcony from which you can watch boats glide by on the river. But the 'Agathe' suite, named after Georges' grandmother, is the most enchanting of all. On ochre-coloured walls hang family portraits. The bed is romantically placed in an alcove beneath a wooden beam. In the bathroom, rough stone walls, a beautiful niche featuring a washbasin and an antique mirror in an elaborate frame, add a touch of poetry.

I have a long, soothing bath, my privacy assured by two white shutters on the window.

To stroll around Le Chaufourg is to discover a wealth of fascinating details. In the small lounge of the Mansart pavilion, by the open fire, stands a piano with a pile of Mozart scores, inviting you to play. The gardens with their wonderful hedges, designed by Tobie Loup de Viane, are a delight. The lawn is beautifully soft and velvety green lawn, and offers plenty of opportunity for the two resident dogs, Divine and Bagdad Café, to play. The water of the swimming pool reflects the azure blue of the sky and lends an extra dimension to the garden. Everywhere, you can smell lavender. The hedge surrounding the garden is cleverly cut as if it were a terrace. Benches, rustic chairs and plenty of leafy shadows invite you to sit down and enjoy the peace and quiet.

Le Chaufourg does not offer lunch, but Georges Dambier and his cousin Agnès can direct you to plenty of good addresses in the area.

Having dinner at Le Chaufourg is always different: every night, tables are set in the lounge, the dining room, and is the weather permits, in the garden.

Georges Dambier helps me choose from an elaborate menu. I opt for foie gras, duck breast and roast potatoes, and he offers me very special wines from Saint-Emilion, Bergerac etc.

Before I retire to my bedroom alcove, my charming host advises me on the many walks I might consider taking tomorrow: Les Eyzies, Sarlat, Domme, Trémolat and Bergerac, to name but a few.

Georges Dambier converted his childhood home into a poetic guest house.

CHÂTEAU DE NIEUIL

16270 Nieuil   pag. 10
Tel. (33) (0) 5 45 71 36 38
Fax (33) (0) 5 45 71 46 45
e-Mail: nieuil@relaischateaux.fr
Website: www.relaischateaux.fr/nieuil

- **Room amenities:** rooms = 11 apartments = 3
- **Facilities:** Swimrning pool, tennis, lake (fishing), art gallery, walks, mountain biking.
- **Activities in the vicinity:** Golf, horse riding.
- **Sightseeing:** Cognac, Limoges, Angoulème, Roman churches, castles, medieval sites.
- **Credit cards:** Amex, Visa, MC, DC, JCB...

- **Restaurant:** Open every day. Menus ff 250, ff 295, ff 340 and à la carte.
- **Season:** The end of April to the beginning of November.
- **Affiliation:** Relais & Châteaux.
- **Accolades:** 1* Michelin, 16/20
- **Location:** in the countryside, in a park, 4km off the RN 141 Angoulème/ Limoges, next to Suaux

LE VIEUX LOGIS

Le Bourg   pag. 16
24510 Trémolat
Tel. (33) (0) 5 53 22 80 06
Fax (33) (0) 5 53 22 84 89
e-Mail: vieuxlogis@relaischateaux.fr
Website: www.relaischateaux.fr/vieuxlogis

- **Room amenities:** 26.
- **Facilities:** TV, minibar, direct phone.
- **Activities on property:** Swimming pool, walking, mountain biking.
- **Activities in the vicinity:** Canoeing, kayak, tennis, horse riding.
- **Sightseeing:** Castles in the valley of the Dordogne, Sarlat, cloisters and manor houses, prehistoric caves (Lascaux and Font de Gaume).
- **Credit cards:** CB, Visa, Diners, Mastercard, Amex.
- **Restaurant:** Yes.

- **Season:** Open all year round.
- **Affiliation:** Relais & Châteaux.
- **Location:** in the middle of Périgord Noir. Take the highway from Paris to Poitiers, direction Angoulème, Périgueux, Le Bugue, Trémolat. From Bordeaux head direction Bergerac. Then Sarlat 5 km.

LES LOGES DE L'AUBERGADE

52, Rue Royale   p. 22
47270 Puymirol
Tel. (33) (0) 5 53 95 31 46
Fax (33) (0) 5 53 95 33 80
e-Mail: trama@aubergade.com
Website: www.aubergade.com

- **Room amenities:** 11
- **Facilities:** All comforts, garage, air conditioning, room for disabled.
- **Activities on property:** Jacuzzi, jogging, round trips, cycling.
- **Activities in the vicinity:** Swimming pool (500 m), tennis (2 kms), golf (10 kms), horse riding (6 kms), walking, Walibi, ULM, waterskiing.
- **Sightseeing:** Manor houses & castles, round trips, museums.
- **Credit cards:** AE, DC, CB, Visa, Eurarcard.
- **Restaurant:** Gastronomical.
- **Season:** From April 1 to October 31.

- **Affiliation:** Relais & Châteaux, Relais Gourmand, Maître Cuisinier de France, Eurotoques.
- **Location:** Airport Agen (1 km), airport Toulouse/ Blagnac (90 kms) and airport Bordeaux (135 kms). From Toulouse: A62, turn off Valence d'Agen, direction Golfech, Lamagistère via the N 113, then D20 and D248. From Bordeaux: A62, direction Agen, Toulouse via the N 113 to Lafox then the D16

CHÂTEAU DES VIGIERS

24240 Monestier   p. 26
Tel. (33) (0) 5 53 61 50 00
Fax (33) (0) 5 53 61 50 20
e-Mail: reservevigiers@calva.net
Website: www.vigiers.com

- **Room amenities:** 36 rooms + 11 junior suites.
- **Facilities:** Satellite TV, mini-bar, safe.
- **Activities on property:** Golf, tennis, fishing, mountain biking, swimming pool, body treatment.
- **Activities in the vicinity:** horse riding, ballooning.
- **Sightseeing:** Visit to vineyards, wine tastings, medieval sites and manor houses. Lascaux caves, valley of the Dordogne.
- **Credit cards:** Amex, Visa, Eurocard, Mastercard, Diners.

- **Restaurant:** Gastronomical "Les Fresques", brasserie "Le Chai".
- **Season:** Closed in January and February.
- **Affiliation:** S.L.H., Virgin Hotels, Warwick.
- **Accolades:** Guide Michelin.
- **Location:** Dordogne, Périgord, 1h from Bordeaux. D18 between Ste-Foy-La-Grande and Eymet.

MOULIN DU ROC

- **Room amenities:** 12 rooms - 1 apartment.
- **Facilities:** TV, minibar, airconditioning and balnéo bathing in several rooms, direct telephone line.
- **Activities on property:** Tennis, swimming pool, fishing, walking in the park.
- **Activities in the vicinity:** Golf (18 holes), karting, canoeing/ kayak, cycling, horse riding. Sightseeing:Casties, caves, museums...
- **Credit cards:** Visa, Mastercard, American Express, Diners Club, JCB.
- **Restaurant:** Lunch menu during weekdays at ff 170. Menus at ff 250, ff 320 and ff 430 + á la carte.

24530 Champagnac de Belair   p. 32
Tel. (33) (0) 5 53 02 86 00
Fax (33) (0) 5 53 54 21 31

- **Season:** Open beginning of March to January 1 the following year.
- **Affiliation:** independant.
- **Location:** Brantóme (6 km) by the river Dronne. Highway A10 Paris/ Angoulème. Brantóme at 25 kms from Périgueux. In Brantóme: to Champagnac de Belair.

CHÂTEAU CORDEILLAN-BAGES

- **Room amenities:** 24 + 1 junior suite.
- **Activities on property:** L'Ecole du Bordeaux.
- **Activities in the vicinity:** Tennis, swimming pool (500 m), horse riding (8 kms), golf (7 courses within a distance of 40 kms).
- **Sightseeing:** Roman and gothic churches, castles, wine tastings. Ocean and lakes, forest.
- **Credit cards:** Amex, Diners, Visa, Eurocheques.
- **Restaurant:** Yes, except Saturday at noon and Monday all day. Dining al fresco on the terrace weather permitting.
- **Season:** From April 1 up to October 30.

Route des Châteaux   p. 38
33250 Pauillac
Tel. (33) (0) 5 56 59 24 24
Fax (33) (0) 5 56 59 01 89
e-Mail: cordeillan@relaischateaux.fr
Website: http/www.integra.fr/relais-chateaux/cordeillan

- **Open:** from February 1 to December 15.
- **Season:** From April 1 up to October 30.
- **Affiliation:** Relais & Châteaux.
- **Accolades:** Michelin star, 16/20 Gault & Millau. 17th century cloister. 4 stars.
- **Location:** Among vineyards .A10 - turn off Nr7 then the N215 direction St-Laurent and the D206 direction Pauillac.

CHÂTEAU DE MERCUÈS

- **Room amenities:** 22 rooms (ff 850 to ff 1.500) - 8 suites (ff 1.500 to ff 2.250)
- **Activities on property:** Swimming pool (25 m x 12 m), tennis (2 courts), visits to wine cellars and wine production. Wine tasting.
- **Activities in the vicinity:** Golf (30 km)
- **Sightseeing:** Rocamadour, Sarlat, Vallée de la Dordogne, Valley of Lot.
- **Credit cards:** CB, Mastercard, Diners, Amex, JCB.
- **Restaurant:** 1 Michelin star, 15/20 Gault & Millau. Closed Mondays (all day) and at noon Tuesdays (except July and August)
- **Season:** Open from Easter to All Saints'Day.

46090 Mercues – Cahors   p. 42
Tel. (33) (0) 5 65 20 00 01
Fax (33) (0) 5 65 20 05 72
e-Mail: mercues@relaischateaux.fr
Website: www.relaischateaux.fr/mercues

- **Affiliation:** Relais & Châteaux (4 stars).
- **Accolades:** Former Archbishop residence.
- **Location:** Facing valley of the Lot river and the famous vineyards of Cahors. A62 Bordeaux-Toulouse, turn off Montauban, A20 Cahors, D911, Mercuès or A 20 Paris-Cahors Nord N 20. D 911 Mercues

---

SAINT-JAMES

- **Room amenities:** 15 standard rooms, 3 American suites (one with jacuzzi and terrace).
- **Facilities:** 2 rooms for handicapped with an elevator.
- **Activities on property:** Heated swimming pool, private parking, sauna. Tennis in the village, walking in the forest.
- **Activities in the vicinity:** Visit several castles and Bordeaux, golf, horse riding, cycling.
- **Sightseeing:** monuments, exhibitions...
- **Credit cards:** Mastercard, Visa, Amex, Diners.
- **Restaurant:** Saint-James (gastronomical), Bistroy (brasserie), Café de l'Espérance (rôtisserie).
- **Season:** Low season from November 1 up to March 31. High season from April 1 up to October 31.

3, Place Camille Hostein   p. 48
33270 Bouliac
Tel. (33) (0) 5 57 97 06 00
Fax (33) (0) 5 56 20 92 58
e-Mail: stjames@atinternet.com
Website: http://www.jm-amat.com

- **Affiliation:** Relais & Châteaux.
- **Accolades:** Jean-Marie Amat.
- **Location:** 5 km east of Bordeaux. Turn off at n°23 Bouliac onto the parallel minor road, turn right at the first lights, left at the second lights and pass the "Gendarmerie Mobile". Once up the hill, turn right direction church. The hotel is facing the post office in the village square.

DOMAINE D'AURIAC

- **Room amenities:** 26 rooms.
- **Facilities:** Secure private parking, garden, terrace, rooms with air conditioning, restaurant with air conditioning, elevator.
- **Activities on property:** Swimming pool, tennis, golf 18 holes.
- **Activities in the vicinity:** Horse riding, watersports, squash.
- **Sightseeing:** The medieval city of Carcassonne, Cathar castles, abbeys and the Canal du Midi.
- **Credit cards:** CB, AE, MC, DC, Visa.
- **Restaurant:** Yes, regional and traditional cuisine.

Route de Sainte-Hilaire   p. 56
Carcassonne
Tel. (33) (0) 4 68 25 72 22
Fax (33) (0) 4 68 47 35 54
e-Mail: auriac@relaischateaux.fr
Website: http://www/relaischateaux.fr

- **Season:** High season : Easter to November. Low season: December to Easter.
- **Affiliation:** Relais & Châ-teaux.
- **Location:** in a park of 4 ha, 5 min from medieval Carcassonne. A61 turn off "Carcassonne-Ouest". Direction Centre Hospitalier.

LE COUVENT DES HERBES, LES PRÉS D'EUGÉNIE & LA FERME THERMALE D'EUGÉNIE

- **Room amenities:** in the Convent: 4 rooms and 4 apartments. In Les Prés d'Eugénie: 12 rooms and 3 apartments.
- **Facilities:** All rooms with TV, minibar, direct phone line, private safe.
- **Activities on property:** Spa in La Ferme Thermale d'Eugénie, swimming pool.
- **Activities in the vicinity:** Tourist trips through the Tursan wine district.
- **Sightseeing:** Lourdes (pilgrimage). Tour of the bastides. Visits to abbeys.
- **Credit cards:** All major cards accepted.

40320 Eugénie-les-Bains   p. 60
Tel. (33) (0) 5 58 05 06 07
Fax (33) (0) 5 58 51 10 10
e-Mail: guerard@relaischateaux.fr
Website: www.michelguerard.com

- **Restaurant:** Low calorie cuisine and gourmet cuisine in Les Prés d'Eugénie and local specialties in La Ferme aux Grives.
- **Season:** February 15 up to December 1 (the Convent is also open 23/12 to 01/01).
- **Affiliation:** Relais & Châteaux.
- **Location:** Aquitaine (the south-west of France). Motorway Bordeaux/ Toulouse. Turn off at Aiguillon. Direction Mont-de-Marsan, Grenade-sur-Adour. Helipad. Airport: Bordeaux 120 km, Pau 45 km, Toulouse 150 km. Train stations: Pau TGV at 45 km, Dax at 75 km, Mont-de-Marsan at 27 km.

LA MAISON ROSE

- **Rooms:** 27 rooms, 5 fully equipped studios.
- **Facilities:** All rooms with TV and direct phone line.
- **Activities on property:** Spa in La Ferme Thermale, swimming pool.
- **Activities in the vicinity:** Tourist trips in the Tursan wine district.
- **Sightseeing:** Lourdes (pilgrimage). Tour of the bastides. Visits to abbeys.
- **Credit cards:** All major cards accepted.
- **Restaurant:** Low calorie cuisine and gourmet cuisine in Les Prés d'Eugénie and local specialties in La Ferme aux Grives.

40320 Eugénie-les-Bains   p. 70
Tel. (33) (0) 5 58 05 06 07
Fax (33) (0) 5 58 51 10 10
e-Mail guerard @relaischateaux.fr
Website www.michelguerard.com

- **Season:** February 15 up to December 1.
- **Affiliation:** Chaîne Thermale du Soleil.
- **Location:** Aquitaine (the south-west of France). Motorway Bordeaux/ Toulouse. Turn off at Aiguillon. Direction Mont-de-Marsan, Grenade-sur-Adour. Helipad. Airport: Bordeaux 120km, Pau 45km, Toulouse 150 km. Train stations: Pau TGV at 45 km, Dax at 75 km, Mont-de-Marsan at 27 km.

LA FERME AUX GRIVES ET LES LOGIS DE LA FERME

- **Rooms:** 4.
- **Facilities:** All rooms with TV, minibar, direct phone line, private safe.
- **Activities on property:** Spa in La Ferme Thermale, swimming pool.
- **Activities in the vicinity:** Tourist trips in the Tursan wine district.
- **Sightseeing:** Lourdes (pilgrimage). Tour of the bastides. Visits to abbeys.
- **Credit cards:** All major cards accepted.
- **Restaurant:** Low calorie cuisine and gourmet cuisine in Les Prés d'Eugénie and local specialties in La Ferme aux Grives.
- **Season:** February 15 to December 1 and December 23 to January 1.

40320 Eugénie-les-Bains   p. 74
Tel. (33) (0) 5 58 05 06 07
Fax (33) (0) 5 58 51 10 10
e-Mail: Guerard@relaischateaux.fr
Website: www.michelguerard.com

- **Affiliation:** Relais & Châteaux.
- **Location:** Aquitaine (the south-west of France). Motorway Bordeaux/ Toulouse. Turn off at Aiguillon. Direction Mont-de-Marsan, Grenade-sur-Adour. Helipad. Airport: Bordeaux 120 km, Pau 45 km, Toulouse 150 km. Train stations: Pau TGV at 45 km, Dax at 75 km, Mont-de-Marsan at 27 km.

LE PARC VICTORIA

- **Room amenities:** 8 rooms, 4 junior suites.
- **Facilities:** Minibar, safe, air conditioning and marble bathrooms.
- **Activities on property:** Swimming.
- **Activities in the vicinity:** Thalassotherapy at 400 m, golf, deep sea fishing.
- **Sightseeing:** Coast and Pyrénées, Gugenheim museum in Bilbao. La Maison d'Edmond Rostang in Cambo-les-Bains.
- **Credit cards:** Eurocard, Mastercard, Visa, Diners Club, American Express.
- **Restaurant:** Gastronomical restaurant "Les Lierres". Restaurant beside the swimming pool. Season:Hotel open from March 15 up to November 15. Restaurants open from April 1 up to October 31. Tuesday closed in the low season.

5, rue Cepé   p. 80
64500 Saint Jean-de-Luz
Tel. (33) (0) 5 59 26 78 78
Fax (33) (0) 5 59 26 78 08
e-Mail: parcvictoria@relaischateaux.fr
Website: www.relaischateaux.fr/
parcvictoria

- **Affiliation:** Relais & Châteaux.
- **Accolades:** Gault & Millau, Michelin... Bottin Gourmand.
- **Location:** In residential district of Saint-Jean-de-Luz, 350m from the beach and 15 min walking distance from the centre of the town. Highway A63 -take St-Jean-de-Luz North. At the 4th light turn right direction "Quartier du Lac".

LE MOULIN DE L'ABBAYE

- **Room amenities:** 16 rooms and 3 apartments.
- **Facilities:** Restaurant, terrace by the river, gardens.
- **Activities on property:** Mountainbike, fishing (trouth), canoëing (Dronne).
- **Activities in the vicinity:** visit to castles (Bourdeilles and Puyguilhem), caves (Villars), Abbey of Brantôme, typical market on Fridays, village of Saint Jean de Col, winetasting (Bergerac).
- **Credit cards:** Visa, Master, Amex, Diners.
- **Restaurant:** 1 Michelin star, gastronomical (50 seats).
- **Season:** April 29 - November 2.

1, Route de Bourdeilles   p. 86
24310 Brantôme en Périgord
Tel. (33) (0) 5 53 05 80 22
Fax (33) (0) 5 53 05 75 27
e-Mail: moulin@relaischateaux.fr
Website: www. relaischateaux.fr/moulin

- **Affiliation:** Relais & Châteaux.
- **Accolades:** 3 romantic houses: Le Moulin, La Maison du Meunier, La Maison de l'Abbé.
- **Location:** By the river Dronne. Bordeaux airport 120 km, Périgueux National 25 km.

CHÂTEAU DE PUY ROBERT

- **Room amenities:** 38.
- **Activities on property:** Heated outdoor pool, mountain biking.
- **Activities in the vicinity:** Canoeing, kayak, tennis, golf, horse riding.
- **Sightseeing:** Lascaux, Les Eyzies, Sarlat.
- **Credit cards:** CB, AX, DC.
- **Restaurant:** Yes, 1 Michelin star.

Route de Valojouix   p. 94
24290 Montignac-Lascaux
Tel. (33) (0) 5 53 51 92 13
Fax (33) (0) 5 53 51 80 11 puy
e-Mail: robert@relaischateaux.fr
Website: www. relaischateaux. fr/puy-
robert

- **Season:** May 1 to October 17.
- **Affiliation:** Relais & Châteaux.
- **Location:** in the countryside. From Paris take the A10, then the A71, turn off Vierzon, the N20 Limoges, Brive, the N89 Le Lardin, Montignac.

LA CHAPELLE SAINT-MARTIN

- **Room amenities:** 10 rooms, 3 apartments.
- **Facilities:** 4 stars.
- **Activities on property:** swimming pool, tennis, lake + boat, park 40 ha.
- **Activities in the vicinity:** Golf, horse riding.
- **Sightseeing:** Cognac, Limoges, Angoulème, Roman churches, castles, medieval sites.
- **Credit cards:** Visa, Amex, Eurocard.

87510 Nieul   p. 98
Tel. (33) (0) 5 55 75 80 17
Fax (33) (0) 5 55 75 89 50
e-Mail: chapelle@relaischateaux.fr
Website: http://www.chapellesaintmartin.
com/.

- **Restaurant:** Gourmet restaurant.
- **Season:** Open all year round.
- **Affiliation:** Relais & Châteaux.
- **Location:** 10 min from the centre of Limoges. Coming from Paris A20 turn off at n° 28.

CHÂTEAU DE LA TREYNE

46200 Lacave   p. 102
Tel. (33) (0) 5 65 27 60 60
Fax (33) (0) 5 65 27 60 70
e-Mail: treyne@relaischateaux.fr
Website: www. relaischateaux.fr/treyne

- **Room amenities:** 14 + 2 apartments.
- **Facilities:** Escalator, air conditioning, safe.
- **Activities on property:** Outdoor pool, tennis, park and forest, gardens.
- **Activities in the vicinity:** Horse riding, ballooning, canoeing.
- **Sightseeing:** Rocamadour (15 km), Sarlat (35 km), the valley of the Dordogne.
- **Credit cards:** Mastercard, Eurocard, Visa, Diners, American Express
- **Restaurant:** Gastronomical (closed Tuesdays and Wednesdays at noon + Thursday at noon).

- **Season:** Easter to mid-November + 20/12-3/1.
- **Affiliation:** Relais & Châteaux.
- **Accolades:** Guide Michelin, Gault Millau, Bottin Gourmand.
- **Location:** Looking out over a river. 6 km east of Souillac. A20

MICHEL BRAS

Route de l'Aubrac   p. 110
12210 Laguiole
Tel. (33) (0) 5 65 51 18 20
Fax (33) (0) 5 65 48 47 02
e-Mail: michel.bras@ wanadoo.fr
Website: michel-bras.fr

- **Rooms:** 15 rooms.
- **Facilities:** Rooms: minibar (free of charge),satellite TV, shower, bath.
  Hotel: elevator, bar.
- **Activities on property:** Trekking, moutain bike at the disposal of clients.
- **Activities in the vicinity:** Fishing, golf, horse riding, trekking, bathing.
- **Sightseeing:** Conques, Château du Bousquet, la Forge de Laquide, cheese making.

- **Credit cards:** Diners, American Express, Eurocard, Carte Bleue
- **Restaurant:** Gastronomical.
- **Season:** Beginning of April to the end of October.
- **Affiliation:** Relais & Châteaux.
- **Location:** From Laguiole, direction Aubrac. After 5,5 kms take a left. Follow signs "Michel Bras".

LE MANOIR D'HAUTEGENTE

24120 Coly (Dordogne)   pag. 116
Tel. (33) 5 53 51 68 03
Fax (33) 5 53 50 38 52
e-Mail: Manoir. D.
Hautegente@wanadoo.fr
Website: Manoir d'Hautegente

- **Room amenities:** 15.
- **Facilities:** 2 rooms on the ground floor (1 in the annexe).
- **Activities on property:** Heated swimming pool, river (boat available for trout fishing on private stretch), tennis 1 km.
- **Activities in the vicinity:** Visit to the Lascaux caves 10 km, castles, canoeing, horse riding, golf, gardens.
- **Sightseeing:** Walking, cycling.
- **Credit cards:** AE,Visa, Diners.
- **Restaurant:** Gastronomical.

- **Season:** April 1 to November 2.
- **Affiliation:** Châteaux et Hôtels de France, Relais du Silence, Auberges de Charme, Karen Brown, Good Hotels Guide.
- **Location:** 6km south of the N89 and 25 km west of the N20 (Paris/Toulouse) and between Sarlat and the Lascaux caves. Bordeaux-Genève.

CHÂTEAU DE ROUMEGOUSSE

Route de Rocamadour, Rignac   p. 122
46500 Gramat
Tel. (33) (0) 5 65 33 63 81
Fax (33) (0) 5 65 33 71 18
e-Mail: roumegouse@relaischateaux.fr
Website:
www.relaischateaux.fr/roumegouse

- **Room amenities:** 15.
- **Activities on property:** Swimming pool, mountain biking, cycling, park, walking.
- **Activities in the vicinity:** Golf, horse riding, canoeing/kayak, ballooning.
- **Sightseeing:** Rocamadour.
- **Credit cards:** Visa, Amex, Diners, Mastercard.
- **Restaurant:** Yes.
- **Season:** Easter to December 31.

- **Affiliation :** Relais & Châteaux.
- **Accolades:** Michelin, Gault & Millau, Bottin Gourmand, Hôtels de Charme.
- **Location:** in the countryside, situated in a 5ha park. Crossroad Brivel Gramat. RN140

DOMAINE DE BASSIBÉ

- **Room amenities:** 11 rooms, 7 suites.
- **Facilities:** All comforts.
- **Activities on property:** Swimming pool.
- **Activities in the vicinity:** Tennis (8 km), cycling & mountain bike hire (routes on request). Walking tours. Golf 9 holes (7 km) 18 holes (30 km). Reknowed spa resort (12 km).
- **Sightseeing:** Pau and castle (30 km). Visits to wineries and wine tasting (Armanacs, Madiran, Saint-Mont, Tursan), tours of celebrated porcelain factory, the bastides, museums and other magnificent sites in Gers. Lessons in conservation and tasting of Havana cigars.

32400 Segos (Gers)   p. 126
Tel. (33) (0) 5 62 09 46 71
Fax (33) (0) 5 62 08 40 15
e-Mail: bassibe@relaischateaux.fr
Website: www. relaischateaux.fr/bassibe

- **Credit cards:** All major cards.
- **Restaurant:** Yes.
- **Season:** The end of March up to the end of December.
- **Affiliation:** Relais & Châteaux.
- **Accolades:** All guides.
- **Location:** South-west France, countryside. Axe Bordeaux-Pau-Spain: 35 km north of Pau, 8 km south of Aire/Adour; D260 Ségos.

LE CHÂTEAU DE CASTEL NOVEL

- **Room amenities:** 27 in the castle - 10 in the cottage.
- **Facilities:** Air conditioning.
- **Activities on property:** Tennis, swimming pool, golf practice 3 holes, cycling.
- **Activities in the vicinity:** Canoeing, karting, golf 18 holes (15 min), aviation.
- **Sightseeing:** Collognes-la-Rouge, Turenne Rocamadour, Sarlat, Caves of Lascaux, Les Eyzies, Pompadour.

19240 Varetz   p. 132
Tel. (33) (0) 5 55 85 00 01
Fax (33) (0) 5 55 85 09 03
e-Mail: novel@relaischateaux.fr
Website:
www.integra.fr/relaischateau/novel

- **Credit cards:** Amex, Visa, Diners, Eurocard.
- **Restaurant:** Gastronomical.
- **Season:** May 1 to October 30.
- **Affiliation:** Relais & Châteaux.
- **Accolades:** Michelin, Gault & Millau, Bottin Gourmand.
- **Location:** In the countryside (10 kms from Brive). In Brive take the D901 to Varetz (5 km)

DOMAINE DE ROCHEBOIS

- **Room amenities:** 40 rooms (including 6 apartments).
- **Activities on property:** Golf 9 holes, swimming pool, fitness, billiards
- **Activities in the vicinity:** Canoeing on the Dordogne, tennis, ballooning.
- **Sightseeing:** Lascaux caves, manor houses, medieval cities, castles...
- **Credit cards:** Amex, Visa, Mastercard, Diners.
- **Restaurant:** Gastronomical.

Route de Montfort   p. 138
24200 Vitrac - Sarlat
Tel. (33) (0) 5 53 31 52 52
Fax (33) (0) 5 53 29 36 88
e-Mail: info@rochebois.com
Website: http://www.rochebois.com

- **Season:** April till the end of October.
- **Affiliation:** Small Luxury Hotels of the World, Châteaux & Hôtels de France.
- **Accolades:** Gault & Millau, Bottin Gourmand, Michelin...

CHÂTEAU DE RIELL

- **Room amenities:** 28 double rooms (including 2 junior suites and 3 suites).
- **Facilities:** TV, telephone, airconditioning, minibar, safe, laundry/dry cleaning.
- **Activities on property:** Heated outdoor pool, park (3 ha), bar, helipad, playground, wine tastings, cycle rental.
- **Activities in the vicinity:** Tennis, golf, horse riding, ballooning, wine tastings in the castles.
- **Sightseeing:** Saint-Emilion, the vineyards, boating on the Dordogne, Bordeaux.
- **Credit cards:** Amex, Diners, CB, JGB, EC.
- **Restaurant:** Gastronomical.
- **Season:** April 1 up to October 31.
- **Affiliation:** Small Luxury Hotels of the World, Châteaux et Hôtels de France.

Molitg-les-Bains   p. 144
66500 Prades
Tel. (33) (0) 4 68 05 04 40
Fax (33) (0) 4 68 05 04 37
e-Mail: riell@relaischateaux.fr
Website: www.relaischateaux.fr/riell

- **Accolades:** Guide Michelin, Gault Millau, Guide Hubert, Guide Champérard.
- **Location:** Among the vineyards of St-Emilion, 3 min. from the medieval town and 30 min from Bordeaux. 40min from the airport of Bordeaux, 5 min from the TGV station of Libourne, at the D243 Libourne/ St-Emilion.

HÔTEL-CHÂTEAU GRAND BARRAIL

- **Room amenities:** 28 double rooms (including 2 junior suites and 3 suites).
- **Facilities:** TV, telephone, airconditioning, mini-bar, safe, laundry/dry cleaning.
- **Activities on property:** Heated outdoor pool, park (3ha), bar, helipad, playground, wine tastings, cycle rental.
- **Activities in the vicinity:** Tennis, golf, horse riding, ballooning, wine tastings in the castles.
- **Sightseeing:** S aint-Emilion, the vineyards, boating on the Dordogne, Bordeaux.
- **Credit cards:** Amex, Diners, CB, JCB, EC.
- **Restaurant:** Gastronomical.
- **Season:** April 1 up to October 31.

Lamarzelle-Figeac   p. 150
Route de Libourne
33330 Saint-Emilion
Tél. (33) (0) 5 57 55 37 00
Fax (33) (0) 5 57 55 37 49
e-Mail: hotel_ch@grand-barrail.com
Website: www.grand-barrail.com

- **Affiliation:** Small Luxury Hotels of the World, Châteaux et Hôtels de France.
- **Accolades:** Guide Michelin, Gault Millau, Guide Hubert, Guide Champérard.
- **Location:** Among the vineyards of St-Emilion, 3min. from the medieval town and 30 min from Bordeaux. 40min from the airport of Bordeaux, 5 min from the TGV station of Libourne, at the D243 Libourne/ St-Emilion.

LE CHAUFOURG-EN-PÉRIGORD

- **Rooms:** 9 rooms (including 2 suites), direct phone line, TV, 4 with minibar and 5 with air conditioning.
- **Facilities:** Lounges, billiards piano, swimming pool, boating, secure parking at night.
- **Activities in the vicinity:** Tennis 1 km, 2 golf courses 18 holes (Domaine de Saltgourde, Château des Vigiers), 1 golf course 9 holes (Domaine de la Lande), horse riding.
- **Sightseeing:** Saint-Emilion, Aubeterre and the forest of La Double, Roman itinerary, Brantôme, Bergerac, Périgueux, Hautefort, Lascaux caves, Sarlat, Domme.

"Le Chaufourg"   p. 158
24400 Sourzac (Dordogne)
Tel. (33) (0) 5 53 81 01 56
Fax (33) (0) 5 53 82 94 87
e-Mail: chaufourg.hotel@wanadoo.fr

- **Credit cards:** Amex, Visa, Eurocard, Mastercard, Diners.
- **Restaurant:** Only for residents (reservation requested).
- **Season:** Open all year round (in the winter on request)
- **Location:** 30 km south-west of Périgueux via the N89, direction Mussidan.

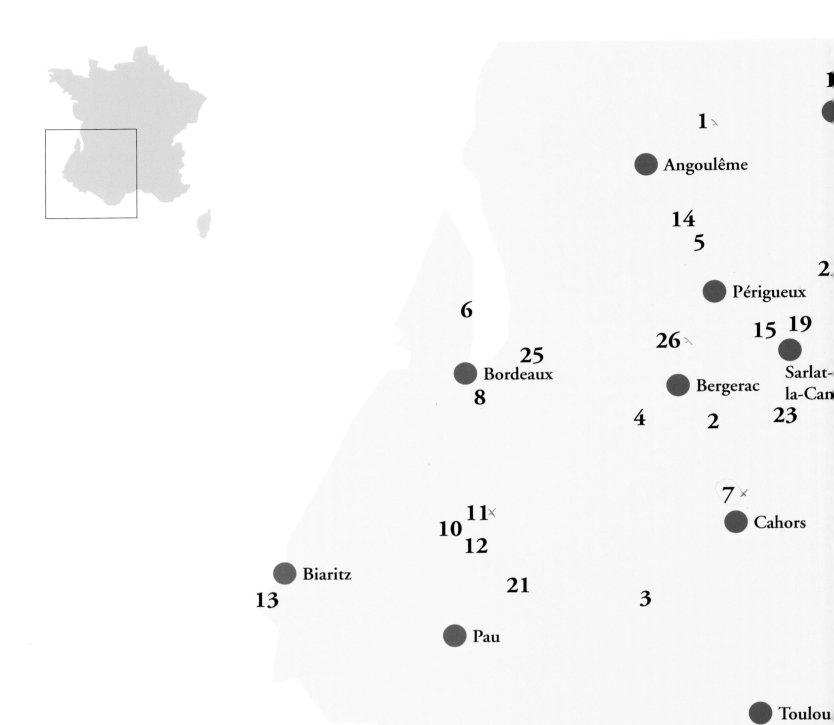

1

14

5

Périgueux

2.

6

26

15 19

25

Bordeaux

Bergerac

Sarlat-
la-Can

8

4   2   23

7

11

Cahors

10

12

21

3

Biaritz

13

Pau

Toulou

Angoulême

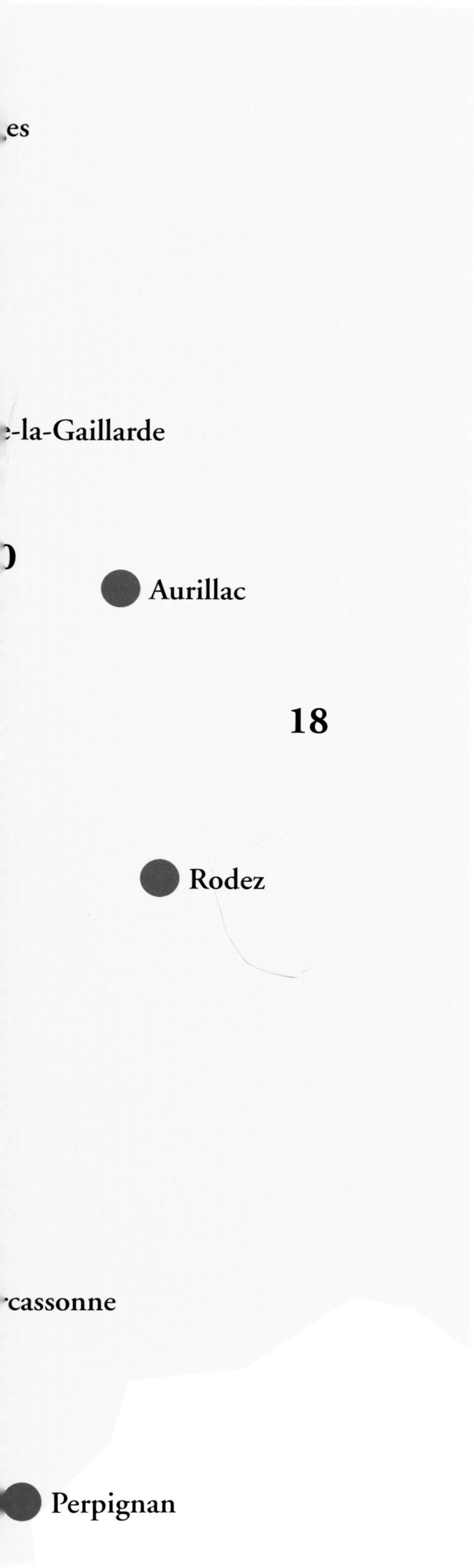

es

-la-Gaillarde

0

● **Aurillac**

18

● **Rodez**

cassonne

● **Perpignan**

Published in this series

Hidden Gems of Provence

Editions in English, French,
German and Dutch.